A Travelling People's Feild Guide

Originating from
RESHAD FEILD

and developed by
MATTHEW SHOEMAKER

Bloomington, IN　　　　　Milton Keynes, UK

AuthorHouse™
1663 Liberty Drive, Suite 200
Bloomington, IN 47403
www.authorhouse.com
Phone: 1-800-839-8640

AuthorHouse™ UK Ltd.
500 Avebury Boulevard
Central Milton Keynes, MK9 2BE
www.authorhouse.co.uk
Phone: 08001974150

© 2006 Reshad Feild. All rights reserved.

No part of this book may be reproduced, stored in a retrieval system, or transmitted by any means without the written permission of the author.

First published by AuthorHouse 6/20/2006

ISBN: 1-4259-2558-8 (sc)

Printed in the United States of America
Bloomington, Indiana

This book is printed on acid-free paper.

First published in Great Britain in 1986
By Element Books Ltd.
Longmead, Shaftesbury, Dorset

British Library Cataloguing in Publication Data
Feild, Reshad
A Travelling People's Feild Guide.
I. Spirituality -- Quotations, maxims etc.
I Title II. Shoemaker, Matthew
291.4PN6084.57/

Reshad Feild

Born to a traditional English family in Hascombe in 1934, Reshad Feild experienced several successful careers. He has worked as a naval officer, a stock broker, an advertising specialist, a pop singer with the chart-topping group, The Springfields, an antiques dealer and a Radionics healing practitioner. In the course of a lifelong adventure, which he describes as a "continual search for ever finer dimensions of truth", Reshad Feild traveled the world extensively and came into contact with the teachings of Gurdjieff and Ouspensky, met with Tibetan Buddhism and its lamas, American Sioux Indians, as well as shamans and masters of the Sufi path. Eventually he met his true spiritual teacher, Bulent Rauf, who himself stemmed from a long Sufi tradition.

In 1973, at the request of Bulent Rauf, Reshad Feild left the United Kingdom for Canada. He had been given certain specific tasks and teachings to pass on from the very essence of Sufism. His first stop was to be in Vancouver, and from there he traveled throughout Canada and the States, setting up groups for those interested in the teachings, as well as spending some time in Mexico. Over the next 30 years he continued on with his function as a teacher, and also published many books, perhaps the most famous of which is titled *The Last Barrier* and which tells of a small portion of his journey with "Hamid" (Bulent Rauf) in Turkey. Before leaving England, Reshad was involved with the establishing of a centre called Beshara in Gloucestershire. It was very well-known at that time, and was visited by people from all over the world. In 1993 he also started a large teaching centre in Switzerland, called Johanneshof, where he would spend over half of each year. The rest of the time he was based in New Mexico. In 2004 Reshad finally returned to live and work in England.

Although Reshad prefers to have no labels, he has been involved with the path of transformation since an early age. But it was not until he met his teacher in the late 60's that he found what is called the Way of Love, Compassion and Service. He also received initiation into the Mevlevi order of the "whirling" dervishes in Konya, Turkey, and helped bring their sacred ceremony to the West. In fact, his whole life has been devoted to the quest for the purpose of life on earth and the unfoldment of the Eternal Truth, which appears and re-appears in the form that is needed and accepted in specific parts of the world, and at the right time.

BY THE SAME AUTHOR

The Last Barrier

To Know We Are Loved

Steps to Freedom

The Alchemy of the Heart

Breathing Alive

Reason is Powerless in the Expression of Love

Going Home – The Journey of a Travelling Man

The Inner Work

Introduction

This unique collection of expressions from Reshad Feild will be a challenge for the reader. In the course of teaching a class or even cooking a meal, Reshad often comes out with a statement that either baffles the intellect or sings in the heart. These have been called 'snippets', as though they were snipped out of the air. If you have the privilege to attend a class, you may even hear someone say to another, "snip it!"

From the many hundreds of these collected gems, I grouped and arranged the ones here in this particular way to best benefit the reader. The content speaks for itself, and each line has multiple levels of meaning.

One may use these quotations individually or in groups, as contemplations or themes to work with for a time. There are many ways to read and use this book, and I welcome you to find your own. Take it seriously, but have fun with it. This is a guide book for those who are travelling on the way of knowledge, through the gates of love, and on to the path of service in this world.

MATTHEW SHOEMAKER

When you know
you don't know
what you don't know,

the divine guidance
has definitely got you
… to the point of perplexity.

Now carry on!

This world is a hunting ground
for knowledge.

If we don't know
we lack knowledge,
we don't look for it.

If we think we know
anything absolutely,
we know nothing.

Watch the gap

between

what you know
and

what you are trying to know.

The trick of insight,
is to remove the point
from which we view.

You know what to do
with your mind?

Put it in your heart.

Ask the question from the heart,
knowing that you are nothing
in the face of Truth.

The most difficult
thing to heal
is a conception
of the Truth,

for it locks the heart
rather than opens it.

Presume
at your own risk!

The most valuable thing
in the world

is to help someone
ask a question.

If you want to help someone,
get them in the question.

Be in the question,
become the question,

and you become the mirror
producing a question.

Real conversation arises
when two or more people
agree to come together ...

in the name of a question.

You can be passive
and entertained,

but to receive answers
you must ask questions.

There is always
a real question
at any one moment,

because there is always
a real answer
at any one moment.

If we are willing
to ask
a question,

we must be willing to hear
the answer.

You receive answers
corresponding to your ability
to use the answers.

Real questions
bring into manifestation
exactly what is
being asked for.

What is the purpose of life on Earth?

If you ask this question completely,
the answer will unfold continuously
for the rest of your life.

When we have the courage
to realize that
life itself is the teacher,

the timeless Truth
lying within the moment
can come forth.

If we listen
very carefully,

we can hear
the moment speak.

Listening inside …
doesn't mean trying to hear yourself
make majestic discourses.

You listen

by keeping the question alive.

What you are meant to be

and what you would like to be

may be very different.

Don't think about yourself!

It backs up on you …
like bad plumbing.

If you don't know who you are
… why think about it anyway?

If you forget to think …

you might
actually remember.

Until you know
who you are,

you are an imagination.

Sacrifice the illusion
of who you think you are,

so that you may come into being.

Being and capacity
are dependent upon your emptiness
of any concept of self.

The dissolving
of the illusion

is the remaining
of the essential Truth.

We make a very different sound

    when the concept
    of who we are
    is shattered.

You are already
what you are searching for,

since

what you are
looking for
is what is
looking.

Recognition of
what really exists
is the first step to living.

That step begins
the process of refinement,
which is the redemption
of all that is unnecessary.

Life is full
when you are empty.

When we are grateful,

light fills our hearts

and we are able to see the world
as it truly is.

Gratefulness is the key to Will —
that is, the One Will,

and the key to gratefulness
is remembrance.

Life itself
is an experiment
to see
if we can come
to fulfilment.

We are given everything we need
to come to fulfilment.

We are given similar situations
until we learn to redeem them

by being awake
to the inner meaning
of the experience,

and not its apparency alone.

Sometimes what we think
is a real experience

is simply
an imaginary copy
of somebody else's
experience.

You can never have the same experience
as another,

because each of us is unique,

and you can never have the same
experience twice,

because each moment is unique.

Pay attention to impressions …
they come to you for a reason.

Don't be hypnotized
by what attracts you.

If we allow our senses
to rule us,

we are caught
in the world of attraction.

Sentimentality is a complete disaster!

It brings us down
from what we possibly could understand.

Emotions are governed
by the patterns of the past.

If you don't get beyond emotions,
you'll repeat your ancestors' mistakes.

And what use would that be to the world?

As long as we are ruled by the emotions, freedom escapes us.

Emotions are not you …

Don't identify with them.

Go beyond emotions!

We must never allow ourselves to be
attached or to be identified,
because this is to place conditions
on our commitment and our intention.

Any form of expectation is a trap.

Every day we are tested with something
that can deviate us from the Truth.
Recognize this,
but don't get too serious about it.

Bad isn't bad
until it meets
its better half.

Problems
are only
unattended situations.

The moment
you recognize a problem …

it will change.

Seeing

changes

what you are looking at.

We can be helped
by what we see:

the mirror reflection
of ourselves.

If one does not wish for the Truth,
the mirror becomes the enemy.

Once we make the step
toward Truth,
it approaches us.

If we run away,
it may snatch us.

On your journey …

be careful
not to get the mud
from your shoes
in your eyes.

In a crisis
we are faced
with what we
have been perpetuating.

When you are in pain,
it's hard to remember
that everything that happens
is to teach you something
and be grateful for it.

Pain is the visiting card
to yourself.

If you can be grateful for humbling
experiences, the next moment you may
be exalted.

We need creative tension
to keep us going
right on through
the gates of paradise.

There is a part of us
that doesn't want to know
what we need to do.

How can you identify
your lower nature?

It's the one that complains.

When you judge
you go deaf,
blind,
and indifferent

and get stuck
in that moment.

Judgement
is like elastic;

it snaps back
at you.

Man is describing himself
when he thinks
he is describing others.

You cannot even see
patterns in others
without first
seeing them in yourself.

The reason we manipulate other people
is that we can't face being ourselves.

There are three walls
that divide us:

envy,
resentment,
and pride.

True healing is to know
there is no separation.

It's all complete
and it's our obligation
to understand it.

All we can really do
is agree to the setup

and then play the game well.

It's our degree of passion
that starts life
every minute.

For God's sake

go out
and do something
for somebody.

Without sufficient interest in life,
you won't know
what you're meant to be doing.

Since we're meant to serve
what's near,

get near
what needs help!

If you are awake,
you will find yourself
in the right place
at the right time.

Once you are
on top of breath,

you will know
what is needed
at any one moment
in time.

Need attracts
from the environment
that from which
the need can be fulfilled.

Through trust and guidance

the right situation
is bound to occur.

Patience isn't passive,
it's actively receptive.

Perseverance is necessary
to learn patience,

and patience is necessary
to have perseverance.

Know that if you are here,
all is given,

and all is given
because you are here.

Being present
is to serve
the space you're given.

We are the servants
of the moment.

We need to love people
into the present moment.

Be in attention
for those
who are not attending.

Let nothing inside
or outside of you
stop you
from being present.

Most of us carry
the past in one pocket
and the future in the other.

We must be prepared
to make whatever sacrifice is necessary

to keep the eternal moment alive.

A child is born
out of the womb
of the moment.

Yesterday
was the birthplace
of today.

Today
is the birthplace
of forever.

If we are truly
in the present moment,

and not being carried away
by our thoughts and fantasies,

then we are in a position
to be free of fate

and available to our destiny.

When we are
in the present moment,

our work on Earth begins.

The hereafter

is here

after you know.

If we don't "get here first" …
the rapturous applause of the angels
might turn into a plugged up
lavatory basin.

The world to come
is ready to enter

the minute we come
into this moment.

Everything is
in a continuous
state of unfoldment

from the future
into the present.

Truth manifests itself
in the way the world needs

and that way is different
at each single moment in time.

Service is the key to Truth,
for Truth lives in service.

Yoke yourself
to the wheel of service,

and the universe
will turn around you.

Whatever we do
can be an example
of the Truth,

and if done consciously,

can help with the healing of the Earth.

Do not under any circumstances
try to copy someone else.

You must have something real for yourself,

and then you have something real
to give to another.

The art of life
is the ability
to pass on something
real and of value.

Never presume
it will get done

without you.

The world of possibility
doesn't exist without will.

The same things
that keep us from posting a letter,
keep us from applying
the secrets of the universe.

Make your mind
your friend,

and time will be
on your side.

We are the people
who can create conscious time,

through the triad of
willingness,
agreement
and commitment.

What is required?

Courage, humility, and patience:

the courage to address authority,
the humility not to presume,
and the patience to wait
until you know what to do.

The choice is ours,
but the answer is God's.

You need some light
to explore the darkness;

otherwise,
you will have to learn
by your bruises.

The moment you give
agreement to something …

you give it life.

We can bring forth
that which is in latency

by putting our attention on it
and giving agreement to it.

In the relative world,
agreement is a stronger word than God.

Agreement
makes the soul
a knowing promise.

The seed of the soul
is to serve.

Find the intention
that lies within,

and allow it
to come forth.

When we commit ourselves fully,

everything we need
is given to us.

Something may start
to build in ourselves

when we ask
the very important question:

"Do I really want to do this
and am I willing to complete it?"

Once you know love
and that love knows you,
then you can make a decision.

Our intention
always goes before us.

It's something
when your physical catches up
with your intention.

Discipline
is the art
of living.

As you work,
so you are
worked on.

You gain energy
from fulfilling
your intention
deliberately.

The energy that comes
from fulfilling a decision
comes out of sacrifice.

The more you make sacrifice,
the more energy
you have available to you.

Now what are you going to do with it?

Will
is like gathering
the harvest
of sacrifice.

Sacrifice becomes an illusion
if we do it for ourselves.

When we give
ourselves up

through study
and through sacrifice,

we can become
the instruments
of God.

Trust.

The amount of help
you can be
is dependent upon
the sacrifice you can make.

Everything you give out
will come back,
but you never know
when or where or to whom.

All the work we do
offers the possibility
of understanding
to all the other people
in the world.

The responsibility is extraordinary.

Once we decide what we want,

what we are willing
to dedicate our lives to,

then we can receive help
from those who support what we want.

When we work together,
keeping the question alive,
it produces a vortex.

None of us can do anything alone.

"I am not alone" …

Let this knowledge
inflame you
at every moment.

We learn to recognize each other
when we know ourselves.

You may recognize the Divine
coming from someone else

while coming through you.

When you know God
in your heart,

you can see Him everywhere.

The heart
is the one point
that's in touch
with everything else.

When you meet somebody
whose heart sings,
it makes your own heart sing.

When we meet in love,
there is first recognition
and then there is response.

And with this response,
a whole pattern of music
starts to resound in our souls.

A brotherhood explains itself
through love.

That rare love
that lies beyond
the world of desire
defies description.

In it,
time and space
are fused in a sense
of mutual yearning,

yet not
a yearning to return
to anywhere
but where we are.

In such love,
sentimentality has given way
to knowledge,
and knowledge to understanding.

Love is pure energy
that needs to be anchored
by knowledge.

Ground love through knowledge.

There can be no knowing
without longing.

Love longs to be known.

When you know
you are loved,
you have freedom.

Every human being
is a spark
that wants to burst
into flame.

Every tree wants to grow
into the light.

All you have to do
is clear the way for it.

Let one human being know
he or she is loved
unconditionally,

and God is freed.

The greatest healing
is in the moment that
someone knows
they are loved
unconditionally.

Take this knowledge
everywhere with you.

If you want to heal,

never impose
your own opinions
or thought-forms.

Listen inside
and you'll know
what they need.

If there is a place
where people feel
they're not imposed upon,

it becomes like a sanctuary.

Once you know
you're loved
unconditionally,

you can help someone else.

It's difficult

until the point
you realize

it's easy.

To be a healer …

be humble
and grateful
to be here.

Healers are not required
to be puritans;

healers are required
to help.

Healing is not just
to get the person better,

but to get them
to face themselves
in the mirror.

Healing
is a precise moment
in time,

and a healer
is a representation
of that moment.

In healing,

if a person is able
to say thank you,
and mean it,

you know they're going to get better.

The one who does not thank man,
does not thank God.

Gratefulness allows
the old cycles to dissolve.

There is nothing wrong
with loving ourselves.

If we're not grateful
that we're alive,

we're absolute twits.

Guilt is not useful.

If you have made a mistake,
testify to it,

know you are forgiven,
and get on with it.

Healing has to do
with forgiveness

and the ability
to allow ourselves
to be forgiven.

It has to do with wholeness.

Forgiveness isn't hard
if you're in the present moment.

If you're not,
it's almost impossible.

Your past is burned
in the fire of the present.

When we forgive someone,

the knots are untied

and the past is released.

Accept with love the flaws
of your friends and enemies,

and you may learn to love
and accept yourself.

If you have not love for all,

you have not love at all.

Love brings the light
behind the sun
into this world.

Spend time every day
loving not only your children,
your family, and friends,

but every human being on Earth;
and then you will do a good job
of helping our planet.

Each person
needs to know
what he wants,

and to pray for it
every day ...

Eventually we want
the knowledge of love,
the redemptive spirit,
to come into this world.

Through breath,

you can bring
anything into yourself

and send goodwill
anywhere on Earth.

Breathe in
the animal,
vegetable, and
mineral kingdoms.

Then breath them out
as light.

You are a lighthouse
for the universe.

Breathe consciously
and you improve
the quality of air.

It's up to you what happens
between
the time you breathe in
and
the time you breathe out.

Keep open everywhere and always …

then breath can pass through you

and thus you can stay
totally in the present moment.

Die consciously
before you die.

Put your life
into a chalice
and pour it out
to the world.

The moment
you die consciously,

at least one child
somewhere in the world

is born in love.

Why don't you help the angels,
for heaven's sake?

... they help you!

Whatever or
whoever you see
when you are in prayer,
let them in ...

they need to be prayed for.

When you're honest
your prayer will sing,

and it will sing the Truth.

If we pray properly,
we are an answer to prayer.

Prayer allows the opening
through which the answer is given,
and allows the answer
to be manifested through you.

When we recognize
One Absolute Being,
prayer becomes
a matter of opening ourselves
in love
so that the flow of life is facilitated.

If you don't know you're loved,
you haven't got the opening.

Don't pray to God,
let God pray in you.

Pray until
there is nothing
but God.

If there is nothing
of us left
but God,

when we say "Be"
it will become.

When we have
perfect confidence

that our hands
are the Hands of God,

He can heal through us.

Peace on Earth
is dependent upon
a sufficient number of people

who are in it
right now.

Don't just think,
but give thought
to useful matters.

There is tons of thought everywhere
which you can put to good use,
but don't think
about it.

Thought-forms are patterns
of fractured light.

Every thought
has a sound,

and every sound
has a weight
of meaning
that goes with it.

Sound and thought
fix
the pattern
of our lives.

Keep your house
clean enough
for God to visit.

Keep your food
pure enough
for God to eat.

Keep yourself clean!

When space
is properly ordered
and prepared,

there is room
for the Spirit
to come in.

We need to define the space
we're going to work within.

Once you define that space,

everything you need
is contained within it.

Wherever we are,
we have unlimited space
to fill up with beauty.

Space without time
would be a void
without possibility.

Time without space
would be a pointless
waste of energy.

Our Lord
is a dimensionless point
of possibility.

We owe it to God
to let beauty
be seen through us,
reverently.

It's how we pay
our natural debt.

When you allow yourself
to be seen through,

it's like disappearing
up your own vortex.

If we turn inside out,
we are the mirrors
of Truth.

The measuring rod of Truth
is beauty.

Truth recognizes itself
in the perfection of beauty.

The essence discovers itself
in the mirror of form.

In order to see anything
in the mirror,

you need to have enough light.

Polish the mirror
of your heart,

and the world
will be filled
with light.

The world
is a reflecting surface
able to produce
a brilliance of understanding.

Light and understanding
continuously unfold
from within themselves.

The whole world
is popping open
with flowers
at any one moment.

Has it occurred to you

that you yourself
are the eye
of the needle?

Index

Knowledge 1
Asking a question 4
Listening 13
Who you think you are 15
Dissolving the illusion 18
Searching and fulfilment 20
Impressions and experience 24
Emotions 27
Identification 29
Problems 30
The mirror 31
Crisis and pain 33
Lower nature 36
Judgement 37
The three walls 39
Passion for life 41
Patience and perseverance 44
The present moment 45
Service 55
Will 59
Giving agreement 63
Commitment and intention 65
Decision and sacrifice 70
Recognition 75
The heart 76
Conscious love 78

Healing	82
Gratefulness and forgiveness	88
Breath	94
Conscious death	97
Prayer	98
Thought	104
Space	106
Dimensionless point	108
Truth	110
Mirror of light	111
Eye of the needle	114

Printed in the United States
59393LVS00001B/53